APATOSAURUS WOULD NOT make a GOOD SPY

by Heather Sadler   illustrated by Steph Calvert

PICTURE WINDOW BOOKS
a capstone imprint

RÉSUMÉ

ARTIE APATOSAURUS

7 Greens Lane
Long Neck, KN 40052

LENGTH	About 70-90 feet (21-27 meters)
HEIGHT	About 15-17 ft (4.6-5 m)
WEIGHT	33-38 tons
EXPERIENCE AS A SPY	It's a long story.
REFERENCE	NOT this guy →

To my husband, Blake - the best partner I could
ask for. You are my favorite adventure. -Heather

For Carole — who knows everyone like an old friend
in five minutes without even being a spy. -Steph

Dinosaur Daydreams is published by
Picture Window Books, a Capstone Imprint
1710 Roe Crest Drive, North Mankato, MN 56003
www.mycapstone.com

Library of Congress Cataloging-in-Publication data
is available on the Library of Congress website.

ISBN: 978-1-5158-2128-1 (library binding)
ISBN: 978-1-5158-2132-8 (paperback)
ISBN: 978-1-5158-2140-3 (eBook PDF)

Summary: Artie Apatosaurus wants to be a secret agent,
but he's much too tall to be secret! He is terrible at hiding,
he can't disguise himself, and he is too slow to chase bad guys.
In fact, being an Apatosaurus is exactly what makes Artie an awful spy!

Image Credit: Capstone: Jon Hughes, 23

Editor: CHRISTIANNE JONES
Designer: ASHLEE SUKER

Greetings! Secret Agent **ARTIE** Apatosaurus here! Well, not anymore, actually. You see, being an apatosaurus is exactly what made me the worst spy ever. It's over for me, and here's why . . .

Secret agents need to use their heads – and not to smash things. They use their heads to think! I have a tiny brain, so using my head to think was a big problem.

It was hard for me to decode secret messages . . .

trick bad guys . . .

and think fast.

WHAT A DISASTER!

5

Agent Bossy tried to teach me how to spy on crooks.
But it's impossible to disguise yourself when you're
one of the tallest dinosaurs in the world!

Instead of spying, I was the one who kept getting **SPOTTED!**

My weight was also a problem, as it really slowed me down. Being slow and bulky did not lend itself to escaping bad situations. And forget about catching the getaway car in time – I can't even fit into the agent's car!

You might say going on a diet would help me, but that's out of the question! I eat almost **880** pounds (399 kilograms) of food a day to stay strong, so I need frequent snacks and large meals. Good spies never leave their posts, but **HOW** can I concentrate on an empty stomach?

Another problem? I don't have fingers,
and claws just don't cut it.

Pick a lock?
FORGET IT!

On top of all of that, none of the spy tools are made for dinosaurs. The binoculars, gloves, and sunglasses are all too tiny. Agent Bossy gave me an earpiece, but it didn't fit my ear! What's a spy to do without his gear? I'll give you a clue – nothing!

I thought I'd be great at keeping watch, but I was wrong again! My neck gets heavy, so looking left and right and up and down is very tricky. I'm just asking for a headache when I hold my head up too long!

Agent Bossy said I was an awful secret agent.
And after looking at all the facts, I had to agree.
But don't worry about me! I already have my
new job picked out. Introducing **ARTIE**,
the professional ice skater!

20

DINO DIG

The answer to each question below is hidden in the art.
Each answer is one word or number. Dig through
the story until you find the answer. Good luck!

1. The apatosaurus lived about 146-157 million years
   ago. What period did they live in? (page 21)

2. Scientists wrongfully classified the apatosaurus
   as what other dinosaur? (page 14)

3. Apatosaurus were herbivores, eating only low-lying plants.
   What did they eat to help them digest plants? (page 10)

4. The size of an apatosaurus egg could be
   compared with what type of ball? (page 6)

5. The apatosaurus could shake the ground
   using what body part? (page 18)

Answer key: 1. Jurassic 2. brontosaurus 3. rocks 4. basketball 5. tail

MORE APATOSAURUS FACTS

» *Apatosaurus* means "deceptive lizard."

» The apatosaurus was one of the largest animals to have lived on Earth.

» An apatosaurus could whip its tail so loud, it could be heard for miles! However, it was a defense mechanism and couldn't actually harm predators.

» An apatosaurus had a very thick neck that wasn't ideal for quick reactions.

DINO DISCUSSION

1. Would you rather be a secret agent or a dinosaur? Why?

2. What characteristics made Artie a bad secret agent?

3. What do you think will happen when Artie tries ice skating?

DINO GLOSSARY

bulky – big

claws – sharp curved parts on the toes or fingers of an animal

herbivore – an animal that eats only plants

SPY GLOSSARY

binoculars–a device used to see things that are far away

decode – to turn something that is written in code into ordinary language

disguise – to hide by looking like something else

earpiece – a device used to secretly listen to something

getaway –an escape